A Definitive Guide to Healing Crystals

By Perry Valentine
August 2021

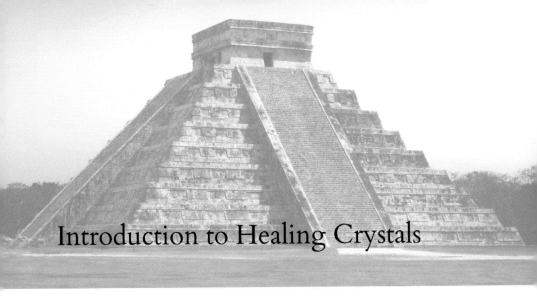

Introduction to Healing Crystals

Crystals have been treasured by mankind since the dawn of civilization. Many cultures throughout human history have valued crystals not only for their beauty, but also their healing properties. Although they may seem small and unassuming, crystals are capable of healing a wide variety of physical, emotional, and spiritual ailments.

The healing properties of crystals are determined by the unique arrangement of atoms in each stone, which is directly responsible for variations in appearance. The color, texture, and shape of a crystal are like a roadmap that guides us to an intuitive understanding of its metaphysical and healing properties. For instance, a blue crystal is often useful for healing diseases of the throat and encouraging communication, which corresponds with the color and meaning of the throat chakra.

Perry Valentine's Definitive Guide to Healing Crystals highlights 15 crystals and the effect they have on the human organism. In three comprehensive chapters, this guide explains how crystals align the chakra system, heal the physical body, and attract love and compassion into the lives of those who use them.

Table of Contents

Crystals for Balancing the Chakras

Crystals for Healing the Body

Crystals for Attracting Love and Compassion

Chapter 1
Crystals for Balancing the Chakras

The seven energy centers of the body are called chakras, a Sanskrit word that translates to "wheels of light." Each chakra is represented by a color and governs a certain aspect of the human experience.

When energy flows evenly through the chakras, health and positive consequences follow. Imbalanced or blocked chakras lead to physical, emotional, and spiritual dysfunction.

A Quick Overview of the 7 Chakras

(7) **The Crown Chakra** (apex of the head): Spiritual knowing and faith in a higher power.

(6) **The Third Eye Chakra** (brow): Perceiving information beyond the physical plane. Intuition and wisdom.

(5) **The Throat Chakra** (throat): Communicating your deepest feelings gracefully. Self-expression and truth.

(4) **The Heart Chakra** (chest): Connects the lower and higher chakras. Your capacity for love, compassion, and inner peace.

(3) **The Solar Plexus Chakra** (stomach): Self-worth, confidence, courage, and mental activity.

(2) **The Sacral Chakra** (lower abdomen): Relating to your emotions and the emotions of others. Pleasure and sexuality.

(1) **The Root Chakra** (base of the spine): Your foundation, basic survival needs, and capacity for independence.

Crown Chakra

Third Eye Chakra

Throat Chakra

Heart Chakra

Solar Plexus Chakra

Sacral Chakra

Root Chakra

① Tiger's Eye

♊ Gemini · I shift my perspective to find my power

Tiger's eye was used in the eyes of ancient Egyptian deity statues because it was believed to grant omniscience. Varieties of tiger's eye include Arizona tiger's eye, California tiger's eye, tiger iron, and hawk's eye.

This reddish-brown and gold stone activates the solar plexus chakra, as well as the root and sacral chakras, and it brings them into harmony with each other.

Spiritual Energy
This crystal resonates with the frequency of the earth. Its energy is grounding and centering, and it is often used to attract money and success into the lives of those who wear it.

Emotional Energy
Tiger's Eye alleviates depression and self-defeating thoughts by teaching us to shift our perspective relative to ourselves and our circumstances. It releases hidden fears and puts us in touch with our own power. In ancient times, it was taken into battle to bring courage, focus, and strength to its bearer.

Physical Energy
Tiger's eye supports a healthy skeletal system, and it is said to strengthen bones that are weak or broken. It supports digestive health, and because tiger's eye also targets the endocrine system, it boosts the metabolism and is believed to remedy thyroid and adrenal ailments.

② Peridot

♌ Leo · August Birthstone · I translate my deepest feelings into action

The ancients felt that peridot's healing power came from the sun, which they believed to be its point of origin. Varieties include chrysolite and olivine peridot.

This greenish-yellow crystal activates the heart chakra and the solar plexus chakra.

Spiritual Energy
The qualities of the heart and solar plexus chakras are merged in this stone. Peridot helps us translate our deepest feelings (heart) into action (solar plexus), which assists us in achieving our life purpose. It is also considered an Elven stone, which means that it brings those who carry it into contact with earth spirits.

Emotional Energy
An excellent stone for facilitating mental focus and endurance, peridot is popular among students and professionals who are required to expend a lot of mental energy. It dispels nervous tension and depression to make way for mental clarity, and it soothes bruised egos, jealousy, and resentment. Peridot helps us relate to others with courage; if you are blocked by negative thoughts or stuck in toxic relationships, this crystal will give you the strength and clarity to break with negative patterns and people.

Physical Energy
Known for its cleansing properties, this crystal is an excellent addition to any detoxification regimen. Wearing Peridot balances the endocrine system and heals the heart, digestive tract, gallbladder, liver, spleen, and pancreas. It energizes the body, brightens the complexion, and brings relief to tired eyes.

4

③ Moonstone

♋ Cancer · June Birthstone · I align myself with natural cycles

Moonstone is closely linked to feminine energy, and it was believed to have a connection to several moon goddesses in ancient times. Varieties include rainbow moonstone, cat's eye moonstone, gray moonstone, white moonstone, and peach moonstone.

This milky-white, opalescent crystal activates the heart, third eye, and crown chakras.

Spiritual Energy
Due to its effect on the third eye and crown chakras, moonstone is a very psychic crystal whose ability to enhance intuitive gifts makes it a popular meditation stone. If you wish to live in harmony with natural cycles, then you will find favor with this crystal. Moonstone protects travellers, watches over pregnancies, and brings good luck to those who carry it.

Emotional Energy
A soothing, motherly stone, moonstone is a great comfort to those who suffer from stress, anxiety attacks, or emotional trauma of any kind. It surrounds us with a calm, clarifying energy that deepens our capacity for compassion and empathy, bringing us closer to the people we love. It's not difficult to imagine why moonstone is considered a "lover's stone" in India, where it is traditionally given as a wedding present. Due to its soothing energy, it's a fantastic crystal for improving sleep and keeping nightmares away.

Physical Energy
Moonstone is one of the best crystals for healing women's issues. It restores the internal cycles and rhythms of the body, and attunes them to natural ones. By balancing the hormones and detoxifying the body, it helps reduce menstrual cramps and stabilize the emotional ups and downs of the monthly cycle. It also helps prevent fluid retention, improves the health of hair, skin, and eyes, and assists the digestive and elimination systems. Considered a stone of fertility, moonstone is believed to help women conceive and maintain a healthy pregnancy. It also improves the quality of sleep, and helps prevent insomnia and sleepwalking.

④ Labradorite

♏ Scorpio · I uncover the truth to find my strength

People of the Inuit believed that labradorite fell from the Aurora Borealis. Varieties include golden labradorite and spectrolite.

This iridescent blue, green, and gold crystal activates the throat, third eye, and crown chakras.

Spiritual Energy

Favored by shamans and healers, labradorite is a profoundly psychic stone that enhances intuitive abilities and brings guidance to those who seek it. Labradorite provides spiritual protection during journeys into altered states of consciousness, and it guards against negative people and influences by shielding the aura and strengthening your energy from within. Its influence extends into the past and future, aiding in the recall of suppressed memories and revealing future events. A stone of synchronicity, labradorite has a way of arranging spiritually important events in your life.

Emotional Energy

Labradorite helps calm the mind and dispel fear by revealing the underlying cause of thoughts and emotions. When the truth is brought to light, there is nothing left to fear but fear itself. This stone brings creative inspiration to artists and a fresh perspective to anyone who feels stuck in a rut.

Physical Energy

Labradorite is a great stone for losing weight because it increases the metabolism. It heals diseases of the lungs and digestive tract, lowers blood pressure, reduces sensitivity to the cold, and improves eye conditions.

⑤ Lapis Lazuli

♐ Sagittarius · I look beneath the surface to find the underlying principle

Ancient Islamic peoples believed that lapis lazuli provided protection from the evil eye. Varieties include denim lapis, whose blue shades are lighter than the common variety.

This dark blue stone activates the throat and third eye chakras.

Spiritual Energy

Lapis lazuli is a visionary stone that enhances psychic abilities and expands spiritual awareness. It is the stone of truth seekers and deep thinkers, stimulating the higher mind and revealing profound truths about oneself and the world. For this reason, it is the perfect stone for journalists, researchers, and psychologists, or anyone working in a field that requires deeper insight into the nature of reality. A fantastic stone for achieving professional success, it encourages decisiveness by giving us faith in our own insights. Lapis lazuli also benefits artists by helping them speak their truth.

Emotional Energy

This stone helps those who wish to discover their true feelings. From repressed anger and trauma to hidden talents and strengths, lapis lazuli reveals what we have not allowed ourselves to express. When we learn to fully embrace everything that we are, it is possible to experience true compassion and empathy, as well as to be honorable and principled with others.

Physical Energy

Lapis lazuli heals disorders of the throat, including problems with the vocal chords, larynx, and the thyroid and endocrine systems. It also improves insomnia, vertigo, high blood pressure, skin disorders, allergies, and inflammation. It is believed that lapis lazuli can also improve the symptoms of Asperger's Syndrome.

Using Your Crystals

To invite health, success, and spiritual growth into your life, try placing a crystal on the chakra or chakras that it activates. Choose a chakra or crystal that relates to prominent themes in your life. Do you feel bogged down by negative thoughts? Try placing a tiger's eye crystal over your stomach. Do you struggle to communicate your thoughts and feelings? Place lapis lazuli over your throat.

One of the easiest ways to balance your chakras is to wear a complete set of chakra crystals. Wearing mixed stone jewelry helps bring the chakras into alignment throughout the day.

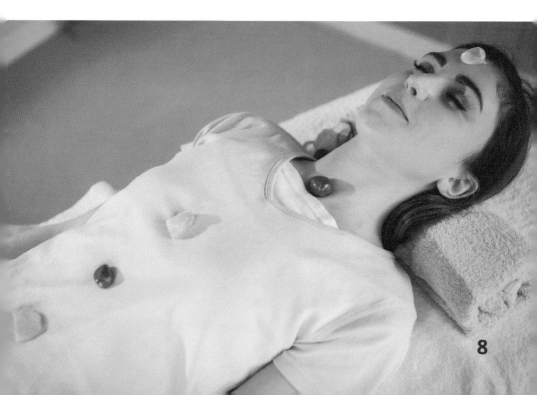

Chapter 2

Crystals for Healing the Body

For thousands of years, crystals have been used to detoxify the body, alleviate pain, and improve disorders of the digestive, reproductive, excretory, circulatory, and respiratory systems. That said, if you are in need of emergency medical attention or have a serious chronic illness, it is essential to seek conventional medical care. While crystals should never take the place of medical treatment, they can be used together to great effect.

The secret to curing physical illness with crystals lies in their ability to direct energy. Exactly how energy influences the physical body is largely a mystery, but some believe that the energy generated by crystals has a direct effect on the nervous system, the expression of the hormonal glands, the way blood flows through the tissues, and perhaps even the electrical processes that occur on the cellular level. These subtle changes cause a chain reaction, the effects of which extend into every physical process within the body.

(1) Amethyst

♓ *Pisces • February Birthstone • I can overcome anything if I know myself*

Valued for its intensely spiritual energy, amethyst was used in the breastplates of Hebrew priests and the burial amulets of the ancient Egyptians. Varieties include brandberg amethyst, chevron amethyst, cacoxenite within amethyst, ametrine, and rutilated amethyst.

This deep purple crystal activates the third eye and crown chakras, as well as the etheric chakras, which are located above the crown chakra.

Physical Energy

Amethyst has a soothing and protective effect on the physical body. Because it regulates the sympathetic nervous system and the endocrine glands, amethyst calms stress-related disorders and improves the quality of sleep. Where there is inflammation, such as arthritis or bruising, amethyst reduces the swelling and expedites the healing process. It is also an excellent stone for building one's natural defenses against disease and infection. Wearing amethyst regularly improves disorders of the digestive tract as well as the stomach, heart, and skin.

Emotional Energy

A stone of sobriety, amethyst grants us the strength to overcome negative thoughts, anger, addiction, and grief by deepening our connection to the divine. Amethyst brings wisdom, creativity, and a deeper understanding of the cycles of life and death. It expands the higher mind, facilitating diplomacy, focus, and the capacity to perceive the root cause of our problems. This crystal is as relaxing to the mind as it is to the body; it calms hyperactivity, and helps stressed and exhausted people find their center.

Spiritual Energy

Amethyst heals by bringing us into direct contact with our souls. For this reason, it is one of the best stones for meditation, and it has been used in rosaries and other religious relics for thousands of years. It opens psychic and spiritual channels within the body, purifying and strengthening the aura to create a protective shield that keeps negative energy at bay. Amethyst heals animals, purifies spaces overrun with negative energy, and protects travellers from harm.

② Topaz

♐ *Sagittarius • November Birthstone • I trust, I focus, I manifest*

Topaz comes in a wide variety of colors, and its healing properties vary widely. Varieties include blue, pink, purple, and brown topaz, white/clear or silver topaz, imperial or golden topaz, and rutilated topaz. Mystic, rainbow, or fire topaz is a popular, multi-colored gemstone created by adding a special coating to white topaz.

Because it is one of the most diverse crystals available, topaz activates every energy center from the base chakra to the etheric chakras. If you want to know which chakra your topaz crystal activates, a general rule of thumb is to apply the color associations of the chakra system (see page 2). For instance, blue topaz activates the throat chakra and golden topaz, the solar plexus chakra. The healing qualities of each stone differ slightly based on the chakras they activate.

Physical Energy
Known as the "gourmet's stone," topaz is often used by connoisseurs of fine food to stimulate the taste buds. It improves eyesight, aids in digestion, and accelerates the metabolism. Because it calms the nervous system and increases blood flow to the tissues, golden topaz is often worn after an operation to bring healing to surgical wounds. Clear topaz is also a great post-surgery stone, and it assists in the treatment of respiratory ailments as well. Blue topaz soothes tension headaches, migraines, jaw tension, and reduces the severity of speech impediments.

Emotional Energy
Topaz brings love, optimism, and good fortune to those who wear it. As fear and depression give way to cheerfulness, confidence, and the desire to put beliefs into action, golden topaz makes it possible to achieve your goals. Blue topaz dispels illusions, aids people in creative professions, and lends courage to those who struggle with public speaking. Purple topaz lessens the symptoms of mental illness and autism.

Spiritual Energy
Topaz works in a general, rather than a specific way. Instead of working exclusively on one area of the body, it directs energy where it is most needed to balance and clarify the aura. For this reason, topaz is a fantastic manifestation stone; as the energy field becomes more focused, it is easier to broadcast your desires energetically. Topaz improves our trust in the universe, brings us into contact with our spirit guides and angels, and helps us receive messages from the spirit world.

(3) Garnet

♑ Capricorn • January Birthstone • I am resilient, I am independent

Derived from the Latin word for pomegranate, garnet is a fitting name for a stone that resembles the small, red seeds of this fruit. This stone was worn by both Muslim and Christian soldiers during the crusades as a warrior's talisman. Varieties include almandine, pyrope, andradite, uvarovite, spessartine, uvarovite, and grossular garnet.

Garnet can be found in a variety of colors. The common scarlet red variety activates the base and crown chakras, drawing the flow of kundalini energy up the spine.

Physical Energy
Garnet has a regenerative effect upon the physical body. It removes toxins, purifies the blood, and helps the body assimilate iodine, calcium, magnesium, and other essential vitamins and minerals. Garnet is useful in the treatment of arthritis and spinal disorders, and it improves the health of the lungs, spleen, and heart. It is an excellent stone for improving physical attractiveness: garnet energizes the body, clears the complexion, promotes weight loss, and increases desire. The ancients believed that garnet could provide emergency assistance to injured soldiers by causing the blood to clot more quickly at the site of a wound.

Emotional Energy
There is no better crystal to have in a crisis situation. The energy of this stone takes a creative approach to situations that would otherwise be overwhelming or traumatic. A crisis becomes a challenge; a traumatic loss becomes an opportunity for a new beginning. This stone brings financial security, success in business, and the ability to stand on your own two feet. It improves self-confidence, increases popularity, and brings luck to those who wear it.

Spiritual Energy
Like topaz, this stone sends energy where it is needed most. It balances the chakras, stimulates kundalini energy, and brings the physical energy field into harmony. Garnet refines survival instincts, sharpening your perceptions of people and situations so you can react to threats instantaneously. Living closely with your instinctual nature builds confidence, removes inhibitions, and the insight gained makes it easier to let go of behaviors that no longer serve you.

④ Sapphire

♍ Virgo · September Birthstone · I remove obstacles to know myself

Sapphire is one of the most valuable stones in the world. Varieties include black, orange, violet, yellow, green, white, pink, and star sapphire.

This gorgeous blue stone activates the throat and third eye chakras.

Physical Energy
Sapphire purifies the body and calms the nervous system, improving sleep and relaxing the body. It is an excellent stone for all conditions of the ears, neck, throat, and head: sapphire sharpens eyesight, improves hearing, and it helps prevent ear infections, sore throats, and headaches. It also works to alleviate fever, fatigue, heart diseases, blood disorders, vertigo, and dementia.

Emotional Energy
Sapphire breaks down the inner walls that prevent us from expressing our true feelings. These walls may exist because we were told directly or indirectly in childhood that we didn't matter, or perhaps we felt like we had to suppress our true selves in order to be accepted by our families. By bringing our true thoughts and feelings to the surface, sapphire lifts dark moods and depression, improves self-esteem, and helps those easily influenced by others to stay true to themselves. This stone brings mental clarity and calm to those who wear it, and it can reduce the symptoms of mental illness.

Spiritual Energy
Sapphire activates the higher mind, and it brings worldly prosperity by helping us energetically broadcast and manifest our desires, often without conscious intent. It is a fantastic meditation stone, connecting those who use it with the spiritual planes, and enabling visionary states, channeling, extrasensory perception, and a sense of inner knowing. Sapphire brings protection, insight, and good luck to those who wear it.

⑤ Onyx

♑ Capricorn · I commit myself to the process of self-transformation

The ancient Greeks and Romans carved images of the gods and goddesses into this stone. Varieties include black onyx, green onyx, sardonyx, sard, chalcedonyx, onyx marble, onyx opal, and rhodochrosite onyx.

This black and white-banded crystal works primarily on the base chakra and the earth star chakra, which lies between and beneath the feet. It is also believed to affect the solar plexus and third eye chakras.

Physical Energy

Onyx is a grounding crystal that builds physical stamina. Wearing this stone reduces recovery time from illness, improves nutrient assimilation, and helps the body regenerate on a cellular level. Onyx heals disorders of the skeletal system, nervous system, elimination systems, and immune system, and it improves the movement of fluids throughout the body. It said to sharpen the senses, especially the sense of hearing, and reduce the symptoms of tinnitus. Onyx is an excellent stone for the legs and feet, calming restless leg syndrome and strengthening weak legs.

Emotional Energy

Onyx tempers extremes, both of a positive and negative nature: it brings flighty people back to earth and moderates the intensity of fear, desire, and anger so that it can be channeled into positive avenues. Commitment is at the crux of this stone, whether it be to a person, goal, or venture. It lends the strength and resilience needed to stick with whatever we set our minds to. Onyx protects us from emotionally toxic environments and ill-intentioned people by creating a protective shield around the aura. It alleviates stress, anxiety, and depression by teaching sound reasoning, wise decision-making, and self-mastery.

Spiritual Energy

Onyx protects and grounds the energy field. Mediums, shamen, and energy healers use onyx because it creates an energetic shield around the aura, preventing other influences and energies from getting into their field while in a spiritually open state. Onyx helps us connect with the energy of the earth, making it an excellent stone for people involved in spiritual practice who feel ungrounded or spaced out.

Using Your Crystals

As a general rule of thumb, increasing the amount of time you spend around your crystals will improve their therapeutic effect. It is also helpful to keep them as close to painful or afflicted areas of the body as possible. To make the most of your crystals, rub them directly on problem areas, meditate with them, place them around your living area, or get in the habit of wearing crystal jewelry.

Kegel exercises are another excellent way to use crystals. They strengthen the pelvic floor and bring healing energy to the female reproductive system.

Chapter 3

Crystals for Attracting Love and Compassion

As recently as a few centuries ago, crystals were used in spells and rituals to manifest true love. Crystals that resonate with the heart chakra facilitate the release of resentment, grief, or any repressed emotion that forms a barrier to intimacy. Defense mechanisms used to keep others at a distance melt away, leaving feelings of kindness, warmth, and generosity in their place.

As the heart chakra opens, it becomes possible to love others more deeply. The art of loving and accepting oneself is the most essential lesson these crystals teach: self-love leads to self-awareness, and self-awareness makes it possible to truly understand and appreciate the ones we love.

① Rose Quartz

♉ Taurus · I am able to love others because I love myself

According to Greek myth, rose quartz was created when Aphrodite cut herself on a briar in her haste to rescue her lover, Adonis. As he lay dying in her arms, their blood ran together over a clear quartz crystal, staining it pink. Rose quartz was found in the facial masks of ancient Egyptians, who believed that it prevented aging.

Its colors range from light pink to rose red depending on the trace minerals found in each stone. Rose quartz activates the heart chakra.

Emotional Energy
The energy of rose quartz is extremely soft, loving, and maternal, and there is no better stone to wear if you are experiencing heartbreak or emotional pain of any kind. Rose quartz is especially healing for orphans, adopted children, or anyone who did not receive the love they needed as a child. This crystal opens the heart chakra layer by layer, dissolving grief, sadness, fear, and resentment to make way for joy, compassion, inner peace, and a positive self-image. It nourishes the emotional centers of the energy body, filling every crevice with love and presence. Above all, rose quartz reprograms the heart to find love within instead of searching for it endlessly in the outer world. As the adage goes, it is only possible to love others once you have first learned to love yourself.

Spiritual Energy
Rose quartz contains the energy of the Divine Mother. Vibrating at the frequency of divine love, rose quartz connects the heart chakra with the Universal Heart. This crystal teaches faith in the kindness of the universe and the fundamental unity of all things.

Physical Energy
The ancient Egyptians believed that rose quartz improved the complexion, and its reputation as an anti-aging tonic has extended to the present day. Rose quartz is said to soothe burns, reduce scars and wrinkles, and return a youthful glow to ageing skin. It cleanses the circulatory, respiratory, and elimination systems, reduces heart palpitations, and prevents fluid retention. Rose quartz also has an uplifting effect on the female reproductive system: it improves fertility, increases libido, and reduces the symptoms of postpartum depression.

(2) Opal

 Libra · October Birthstone · I integrate opposites to realize my potential

Commonly known as the Eye Stone, opal was believed by the ancients to sharpen the eyesight and increase intuitive abilities. All varieties of opal fall under the category of common or "potch" opal, rainbow opal, or fire opal. Specific varieties include Andean opal, black opal, white opal, boulder opal, crystal opal, green or prase opal, matrix opal, milk opal, and moss, water, and wood opal.

This iridescent, milky-white stone activates and connects the chakras to the crown chakra. The chakras activated by this crystal vary based on the colors present in each variety of opal. See page 2 to revisit the relationship between the colors and the chakras.

Emotional Energy
In the same way that opal refracts light into hundreds of tiny, colorful fragments, this stone has a decisive effect on fragmented and repressed feeling states, which are activated and brought to the surface to be integrated. This process can be intense for some, but for those dedicated to understanding their true nature and integrating all aspects of themselves, opal offers extraordinary insight. Because it intensifies inner states and removes inhibitions, opal is an excellent stone for lovers who may struggle to express their true feelings. With the aid of this crystal, it is possible to draw new partners into one's life and connect more intimately with the ones we love.

Spiritual Energy
Opal protects and shields the aura from negative influences and helps its bearer navigate dangerous places and blend into the crowd. Energy workers and shamans make use of its energetic shielding qualities, which allow them to traverse the spirit realm unnoticed. It is an intensely spiritual stone that increases the intuitive and psychic tendencies of those who use it.

Physical Energy
This stone sharpens the senses, especially eyesight, and it tonifies the hair and skin. Opal regulates the flow of water throughout the body, reducing water retention, yet improving the body's capacity for hydration. It purifies the blood and the kidneys, regulates insulin, and balances the hormones to reduce the symptoms of PMS and menopause.

③ Agate

Ⅱ *Gemini • I transform myself through the power of my mind*

Agate received its name from Theophrastus, an ancient Greek philosopher and naturalist who found an agate crystal on the banks of the Acate River in Sicily. Prized by numerous ancient cultures, agate was routinely carved into bowls and amulets. Varieties include blue lace agate, turritella agate, crazy lace agate, dendritic agate, moss agate, laguna agate, and fire agate.

This stone comes in many colors and patterns, although it is generally banded. Its effect on the chakras varies, but generally speaking, this stone stabilizes the aura by transforming negative energy or moving it out of the energy field.

Emotional Energy
Agate is a grounding stone that teaches composure, self-reliance, and practical thinking. Because it removes negative energy from the aura, agate is an excellent stone for releasing the bitterness and anger that remains after the end of a relationship, making room for new love. This stone's practical, clear-headed approach also helps us learn from past relationships so that we can avoid making the same mistakes in the future. Agate provides relief from stress, uncertainty, and trauma, and it brings peace and comfort to those who wear it.

Spiritual Energy
Unlike most crystals, agate resonates at a relatively low frequency. Agate works on the energy field in a holistic way to achieve balance, bringing us into alignment with the cosmos and the world around us. An excellent stone for mediation, agate clears the mind, improves concentration, and encourages contemplation.

Physical Energy
Agate stimulates digestion and reduces the symptoms of digestive disorders. It is said to tonify the cardiac muscles and the blood vessels, improve the health of the skin, and reduce the symptoms of epilepsy. Agate supports a healthy uterus, and it can increase lactation and help reduce the symptoms of postpartum depression.

19

④ Morganite

♓ Pisces · I love deeply because I understand my place in the universe

Formerly known as pink beryl, morganite was renamed in 1911 after J.P. Morgan, a prominent American banker with an interest in the occult. Morganite is a variety of beryl, a family of stones that include green emerald and blue aquamarine.

This pink to pink-peach stone purifies and opens the heart chakra.

Emotional Energy
Like rose quartz, morganite is a crystal of divine love. The energy of morganite has a less motherly, personal tone than rose quartz, however; morganite brings comfort and strength by increasing our awareness of a higher power or spiritual law at work all around us. This stone allows unfulfilled needs and repressed feelings to surface, releasing fear and anger, and helping us face difficult situations instead of running away. It heals old wounds from past relationships, releases defense mechanisms that prevent intimacy, and helps us give and accept love from others. Needless to say, morganite is one of the best stones for attracting a soulmate or improving a current relationship.

Spiritual Energy
This crystal purifies the emotional and spiritual centers so that we can live up to our full potential. By slowly bringing the ego into alignment with the soul, we are transformed by the realization that our lives are part of a divine plan. Morganite opens channels of communication with angels and higher beings, bringing guidance and reassurance from the higher realms.

Physical Energy
Morganite tonifies the heart and nervous system, decreasing the frequency and intensity of palpitations and soothing stress-related disorders. It is also healing to the lungs, throat, and tongue, and it can help decrease the symptoms of asthma and thyroid conditions.

⑤ Jade

♉ Taurus · I manifest love and abundance by turning dreams into reality

Indigenous tribes of the American continent carved jade into masks and religious relics, and it was believed by many early civilizations to have magical healing properties. Varieties include white, red, orange, yellow, green, blue, purple, lavender, brown, and black jade, as well as indian jade.

The chakras activated by the less common varieties of jade vary based on their color. See page 2 to revisit the relationship between the colors and the chakras. Common green jade works best when worn on the heart chakra, which it opens and purifies.

Emotional Energy
Jade is the stone of dreamers, doers, and lovers. It allows repressed wishes and feelings to surface through the stories and images of our nightly dreams, giving us important insight into who we truly are. During the day, this stone helps us take actionable steps to turn our dreams into reality. Jade integrates the mind and body, making it possible to bridge the gap between ideals and the material world, and inviting feelings of confidence and joy into our lives as we accomplish our goals. Jade opens the heart, and it is an excellent stone for attracting new love or improving a relationship that has become dysfunctional. It is also a great stone for anyone who struggles to love themselves because they are perceived as different than their peers.

Spiritual Energy
Jade is a stone of nobility and abundance, elevating noble ideals and increasing the flow of spiritual energy into the material world. It brings wealth, success in business, and a comfortable family life. Jade reminds us to slow down and enjoy the things we've built for ourselves. It lends spiritual protection during energy work and keeps travelers from coming to harm.

Physical Energy
Jade purifies the body by strengthening the elimination and filtration systems. It balances pH and the electrolytes, creating the ideal conditions for health and preventing cramps and muscle spasms. Jade tonifies the adrenal glands, kidneys, and spleen, fortifies the skeletal system, and brings healing to the reproductive system.

Using Your Crystals

To get the most out of your crystals, approach them with intention. Meditating on the heart chakra alone or with your partner will help these stones work their magic. If you're short on time, wear these crystals over your heart or slip them under your pillow at night to increase their therapeutic effect.

Drinking crystal elixirs is also an excellent way to bring the loving energy of these stones into your aura. When a crystal is submerged in water, its vibrations are imprinted upon the surrounding molecules. As you drink the elixir, the energy of the crystal courses through every vein, reprogramming the body on a cellular level .

Thank you for taking the time to read our crystal guide!
We hope it has changed the way you think about these
fascinating minerals.

To read more about the metaphysical and healing
properties of crystals, you can take a look at our blog
on AtPerry's online shop, which features many helpful
articles about a wide variety of stones and their uses.

If you were drawn to the beautiful jewelry in our guide,
you can purchase them on my website,
https://shop.atperrys.com, or just google "AtPerry's".

With love,

Perry Valentine

Printed in Great Britain
by Amazon

66551754R00015